# 9/11

## Through the Eyes of the Lens

### Photography by Alex Matus

Scan the QR code to watch a short documentary about my 9.11 story. Or go to www.alexmatus.com, to register.

No part of this publication may be reproduced, stored in a retrieval system, or transmitted in any form or by any means—electronic, photocopying, recording, or otherwise—without prior written permission, except in the case of brief excerpts in critical reviews and articles. For permission requests, contact the author.

All rights reserved.

Copyright © 2024 Alex Matus

ISBN: 979-8-218-49970-9

The author disclaims responsibility for adverse effects or consequences from the misapplication or injudicious use of the information contained in this book. Mention of resources and associations does not imply an endorsement.

On that September 11th morning, the world woke up to a day that would forever change history. I felt compelled to capture the raw emotions and stark realities of that tragic day through my camera lens.

Inspired by the bravery and resilience of those affected by the events of 9/11, I embarked on a journey to document the moments of sorrow, strength, and solidarity that emerged amidst the chaos. With each click of the shutter, I aimed to preserve the memories of those who lost their lives, as well as the enduring spirit of hope and unity that emerged in the face of adversity.

Through this photography book, I hope to honor the memory of the 9/11 victims and pay tribute to the countless acts of heroism and compassion that unfolded in the aftermath. My goal is to capture the essence of that day in a way that both honors the past and inspires future generations to never forget the resilience of the human spirit.

# 9/11

## Through the Eyes of the Lens

### Photography by Alex Matus

Walking from Home to
# GROUNDZERO
Two hours after the
World Trade Center Crashed

As I moved closer to the downtown area, I noticed a large cloud looming over Manhattan, marking the spot where the World Trade Center had stood just hours before.

The magnitude of the destruction was incomprehensible. The familiar landmarks were now gone, replaced by chaos and devastation.

On Broadway, I joined thousands of other New Yorkers in stunned silence, gazing at the immense cloud dominating the skyline.

We were united in our shock and grief, struggling to come to terms with the tragic events unfolding before us.

Everyone around me was desperately trying to contact their loved ones using cell phones, but the lines were jammed, and communication was nearly impossible.

The streets were filled with a sense of shared sorrow as strangers turned to one another for support.

As I walked further downtown, I strolled on West Broadway in Soho. You could still see the big cloud hanging over the city where the World Trade Center had just collapsed. No one knew what was happening.

A car was parked in the middle of the street with its back doors open, and the radio was playing. Everyone gathered to listen to the news and try to understand the situation.

People stood there in shock, listening to the radio, trying to make sense of the events.

There had been an attack, but no one knew why or who was responsible.

No one could comprehend the scale of what had just occurred. We knew that many lives had been lost, and New York City was under attack.

I continued walking further. A man was sitting on the ground, crying. No one knew the reason, perhaps he had a loved one in the World Trade Center. He sat there, tears flowing. It was a highly emotional sight to witness.

I heard dozens of sirens behind us.

As I turned around, I saw a line of fire trucks driving toward Ground Zero. It looked like an army of fire trucks. They were heading into Ground Zero to rescue survivors, where their friends, the firefighters, had tragically lost their lives just a few hours before.

I saw dozens of FBI agents and possibly over 100 police officers as I reached Canal Street.

They were barricading the street so that onlookers and news crews could not proceed past that point into Ground Zero.

The police officers formed a line and instructed people to vacate the area.

On the opposite side of the street, there was a row of newscasters and reporters.

They were all lined up, seeking clarity
and answers about the recent events.

Before I approached Ground Zero, I passed by Brooklyn Bridge, where thousands of people walked on the Bridge from Manhattan to Brooklyn, trying to get home to their loved ones.

Police and small trucks gathered around. It seemed they were planning the subsequent steps to rescue survivors.

As I looked back, more fire trucks and police arrived on the scene. They were all heading towards Ground Zero. The sirens were deafening, blaring from the fire trucks and some of the police cars.

The first roll of film ended, and I had just one more with me. I loaded the camera and continued shooting. When the negatives developed, I realized the second one was in black and white.

I reached a street where a wall of TV reporters stood.

We could see the cloud, but the reporters were instructed not to go beyond that point; no one could proceed any further.

We stood there in awe, as on the side we were, it was a beautiful sunny day. Just a few hundred yards away, it appeared dark as if it were one o'clock in the morning.

As I walked into the Ground Zero site, the first thing I saw was unexpected. I snapped a photo, finding it hard to believe what I was looking at. This street, usually busy with people and activity, now looked completely different. The scene reminded me of something I had seen in old movies about World War II. I could only see a short distance ahead before everything turned into a scene of smoke, dust, papers scattered on the ground, and a strange smell. It was a terrible smell, a mix of gas, chemicals, and fire.

Suddenly, a police officer arrived on a scooter with a doctor in the back, carrying masks. The officer gave masks to the volunteers who had arrived with me. The doctor told us to put on the masks.

A standard New York bus pulled up, and several dozen firefighters stepped out. The firefighters, or first responders, donned their gear, getting ready to enter the debris to search for survivors.

Left Page: In the midst of them was a captain, speaking and providing directions. Their fellow firefighters had recently vanished beneath the rubble. This group constituted the second wave of firefighters.

The firefighters quietly suited up, forming a large circle around their captain. I suddenly realized I was among them within the circle. The captain cautioned about the risk of gas pipes exploding, advising everyone to be cautious and alert.

Left page: As I walked and took photos, I stood on Broadway, watching the police officers and firefighters come together and do their work. What I saw through my camera lens was unbelievable.

Broadway, where normally so many people are milling about, with restaurants and shops all along the street, now looked completely different—destroyed and covered in debris. The first responders were quietly working amidst the rubble, trying to find people who might still be alive. Papers, metal beams, and dark smoke filled the air. Despite feeling overwhelmed, I kept taking photos. It all felt so unreal, but sadly, it was very real.

While I was taking pictures, I glanced back and noticed a firefighter and a police officer walking into the shadows of Ground Zero just a few feet away from me. I decided to capture the moment because they symbolized something significant that day, something exceptional: the first responders, the real heroes of that tragic day on 9/11.

As we approached the area where the Twin Towers were, I was standing among a few dozen firefighters.

We made a long line and stood there for a few minutes. We just stood there; no one said anything, but we all experienced the same feelings.

I held my camera tightly from anger, mixed emotions, and pure sadness. We all just stood there, and we could not fathom that this incredible, beautiful skyscraper, the mountains of New York, was reduced to rubble, and we were standing a few hundred feet away from it while it was still burning. We just stood there.

The second tower was reduced to a few stories long and was still on fire, burning from the gas and airplane gasoline. The firefighters tried to put out the fires. The first responders looked so small compared to the beams from the World Trade Center surrounding them. The heat was unbearable. I felt like someone had put a small firelight under my skin, slowly burning my body. I could not imagine how the firefighters felt in the heavy uniforms.

A Hilton Hotel nearby had also suffered damage, evident in the holes in its front where debris and beams had penetrated. Some rooms still had lights on, showing they were occupied just hours before.

Left page: I had to pause multiple times, glancing around the streets to confirm if it was all real. My vision was limited to only 100 to 150 yards as I approached each object or intersection. A dark cloud loomed over the site, accompanied by intense heat. Countless papers littered the ground endlessly.

The atmosphere was eerily quiet, almost surreal. I observed an ambulance from Beth Israel Hospital transporting someone, alongside a police car and a fire truck, noticeably damaged and abandoned.

Firefighters, police officers, and EMTs collaborated in another area to search for survivors amidst the massive debris.

Right page: The weather in New York that day was sunny and a bit warm. The area felt extremely hot, with the sky dark and filled with particles.

The large group of firefighters and police officers at the site was impressive. They worked together meticulously, hoping to find people alive.

As I continued taking photographs, the desire to leave intensified. My heart felt heavy, and I gradually realized my camera was trembling. Lowering the camera, I gazed at my hands, noticing the shaking in my left hand holding the camera—a physical reaction to the stress, emotions, and harrowing scenes unfolding before me with each shot.

Breathing was difficult at times. I wore a mask and a T-shirt, while the firefighters wore heavy gear. It must have been tough for them to work through the rubble. Some of them looked tired.

Police officers are gearing up to join the rescue efforts for survivors.

As I departed from Ground Zero, I began my walk back home, passing the spot where the police had set up barricades. Beyond that point, entry was restricted.

Glancing back at the Ground Zero site, I noticed more police officers gathering to enter the area. What had been bright daylight just moments ago now appeared pitch dark.

The contrast was surreal, resembling a nighttime scene despite the sunny day around me.

What had been bright daylight just moments ago now appeared pitch dark.

It felt like I stood between two opposites—good and evil, darkness and light, life and destruction. Taking a few final shots, I lowered my head and made my way back home.

"**In memory of the 3,000 souls who perished that day.**"
**The Day of 9/11**

Scan the QR code to watch a short documentary about my 9.11 story.
Or go to www.alexmatus.com, to register.

## Photographer and Documentary Producer

Alex Matus is a street and portrait photographer with over 25 years of experience. He refined his craft at the prestigious International Center of Photography in New York.

His Powerful 9/11 photo collection is a permanent collection in the 9/11 Memorial Museum, reflecting his deep connection to the event and its impact.

In addition to his artistic achievements, Alex has raised thousands of dollars by donating his photography to various non-profit organizations, including The Michael J. Fox Foundation, NYANA, and NYC Public Schools. His work not only captures compelling images but also continues to inspire and make a difference in support of meaningful causes.